pean
~~aterways
Regulations

The CEVNI Rules Explained

Written by Tam Murrell

Proofreading: Alan Thatcher
Illustrations: Pete Galvin
Photos: Tam Murrell
Layout: Creativebyte
Printed through: World Print

We recommend that you carry the relevant navigation handbook on board for the areas you intend to cruise.

Published by
The Royal Yachting Association
RYA House, Ensign Way,
Hamble, Southampton SO31 4YA
Tel: 0844 556 9516 Fax: 0844 556 9555
Email: publications@rya.org.uk
Web: www.rya.org.uk

Follow us on Twitter @RYAPublications #CEVNI

ISBN: 978-1-906435-87-5

The RYA is committed to encouraging both women and men to participate in boating.
For clarity only, the text in this handbook is written using the masculine gender e.g. Man Overboard.

Foreword

A cruise through the inland waterways of Europe can be an enchanting experience, made much more pleasant by knowing the regulations that are in force for navigation. As pleasure boaters expand their horizons to include the waterways of Eastern Europe, venturing further afield into Poland or onto the Danube, a sound understanding of the rules becomes even more important.

Whilst the delight of 'getting away from it all' is easy to understand, it is essential to do your homework prior to departure and to ensure that you know what is expected of you in advance – to do otherwise might be dangerous and costly! The CEVNI code provides a set of signs, rules and procedures for navigating Europe's inland waterways, many of which are heavily utilised by commercial traffic. Commercial skippers know the CEVNI requirements and will expect other boat operators to know what is going on. Understanding the CEVNI regulations is the best way of protecting yourself and your boat.

The CEVNI code is used as the basis for a number of country-specific regulations which include navigation on the Rhine and in France and the Netherlands. Nevertheless, there are still a number of national variations and visitors to any country will need to make themselves aware of any local requirements. However, as CEVNI becomes progressively more integrated with national regulations, it is likely that many local variants will disappear, and a firm grasp of CEVNI is an essential pre-requisite for anyone cruising on the continental mainland.

A CEVNI qualification and carrying the CEVNI rule book onboard happens to be a legal requirement, but there is no reason why learning shouldn't be easy. This, the latest revision of the RYA European Waterways Regulations book, provides all the information you need in a clear and concise format. The book will make these things crystal clear, enabling a successful CEVNI examination, and is an extremely useful reference book to have on your boat.

Enjoy the book, enjoy the learning and enjoy the cruising on the inland waterways of Europe.

Stuart Carruthers
RYA Cruising Manager

CEVNI (Code Européen des Voies de Navigation Intérieure) is the Code governing navigation on all the interconnected European inland waterways. It was originally devised by the United Nations in 1985 to allow boatmen of all nationalities to communicate with each other and understand what is going on without necessarily speaking each other's language, and is under regular review by the Inland Transport Committee. This book contains the latest revisions at version 4.

CEVNI is the basis for the various countries' own regulations, such as the *Reglement General de Police* in France and Belgium, the *Binnenvaart Politie Reglement* in the Netherlands, and the *Reglement de Police pour la Navigation du Rhin*. Local regulations may differ from the basic CEVNI regulations in some respects when dealing with more specific situations. However, knowledge and understanding of CEVNI is an essential prerequisite for anyone cruising on the European inland waters.

Many of the local variations are included here, but the most notable exceptions at present are Belarus, Kazakhstan, the Republic of Moldova, the Russian Federation, and Ukraine. If you are planning to visit these countries you should familiarise yourself with the many specific requirements in force there. As CEVNI becomes progressively more integrated with national regulations it is likely that many local variants will disappear.

Over the past few years there has been a big increase in the number of pleasure craft using European inland waters. These are often vessels such as narrowboats, wide-beam cruisers, and new-builds or converted Dutch barges, many of which fall outside the definition of Small Craft and are expected to comply fully with the requirements. If they remain in European waters longer than as a visitor they will generally also be expected to comply with equipment requirements, such as having a blue board, which may not have been necessary in the vessel's home country.

Although the rules might look daunting when first encountered they are simple enough in practice. Their fundamental purpose is the safety of all users, both pleasure and commercial.

Definitions

Boatmaster
The person who has all the necessary qualifications and is in charge of the vessel.

Vessel
Any craft on inland waterways including Small Craft, Ferries, Floating Equipment and sea-going vessels.

Normal Vessel
Any vessel other than Small Craft.

Small Craft
Vessels up to 20m long, other than tugs, Ferries, and boats licensed to carry more than 12 passengers. Some authorities use 15m as the cut-off, either generally or for specific waterways.

Motorised Vessel
Any vessel proceeding with its own mechanical means of propulsion.

Sailing Vessel
Any vessel proceeding under sail only. If using auxiliary engine it is considered to be a Motorised Vessel.

Floating Equipment
Floating machinery, such as dredgers, elevators, cranes, etc.

Floating Installation
A fixed floating structure, e.g. floating dock, landing stage, etc.

Floating Material
Any raft or object capable of navigation, other than a vessel or Floating Installation.

Ferry
Vessel providing transport across a waterway.

Convoy
Tug and barges under tow or being pushed, or vessels coupled side by side.

High Speed Vessel
A motorised vessel, other than Small Craft, capable of speeds in excess of 40 km/h in still water.

Scintillating Light and
Quick Scintillating Light
A light flashing 50–60 times per minute and 100–120 times per minute.

Berthing
To make fast directly or indirectly to the bank (moored) or bed of the navigation (anchored). A **Stationary Vessel** is one moored or at anchor.

Left Bank (also Left-Hand Side)
The bank on the left-hand side as you look downstream (downhill on a canal).

Right Bank (also Right-Hand Side)
The bank on the right-hand side as you look downstream (downhill on a canal).

On summit levels of canals, and on broad waterways and lakes, the terms left and right are defined by the relevant authorities. For the purposes of CEVNI, waterways are divided into two classes:
Class 1 Normally the larger rivers
Class 2 Canals, lakes, and broad waterways

The CEVNI rules are intended to enable helmsmen in Europe to interact safely with often very large vessels in extremely confined waters without needing to speak each other's language. This book tries to strike a balance between stating the rules comprehensively and making them understandable to the pleasure boater as a quick, user-friendly and straightforward reference. Whilst all reasonable care has been taken, neither the RYA nor the author can be held liable for any misinterpretations that might occur.

Contents

Boatmaster

The Boatmaster is responsible for the vessel. He must hold all the necessary qualifications and ensure the regulations are complied with at all times. He must be on board when his vessel is under way.

Even in the absence of specific rules, the Boatmaster must exercise vigilance and good practice to avoid damage of any kind to vessels, banks, works, etc.

He must take every step to avoid imminent danger, even if this entails departure from the regulations.

If a nearby vessel needs assistance, the Boatmaster must give immediate aid commensurate with the safety of his own vessel.

Boatmaster and crew must not navigate if their abilities are impaired by tiredness or intoxication.

Crew

Crew members must carry out the Boatmaster's orders and assist in compliance of the regulations.

There must be sufficient skilled crew to ensure the safety of the vessel and everyone on board.

The helmsman must be suitably qualified and over 16 years old (21 for High Speed Vessels,18 for vessels over 20m in France).

Vessels

A vessel's dimensions and speed must be suitable for the waterway it is on. It should not be overloaded in any way. It must carry adequate life-saving devices for all persons on board.

The helmsman must have a clear view in all directions and be able to hear sound signals. If necessary, fit mirrors for clear, all-round visibility. If circumstances require it, a look-out must be posted. The helmsman must be able to communicate with crew positions at all times.

The ship's registration documents, national or European Community safety certificate, the Boatmaster's licence (e.g. ICC), and a current copy of the regulations for the relevant waterways must be kept on board and available for inspection.

Some countries require Normal Vessels to keep a log.

The vessel's name and registry details should be marked indelibly fore and aft on the outside of the hull in letters at least 20cm high (10cm letters on the outside, for Small Craft). The owner's name and registry address should be displayed conspicuously. Tenders must be identified. On Normal Vessels, anchors must be indelibly marked with the name of the vessel. The national ensign should be flown when under way by day.

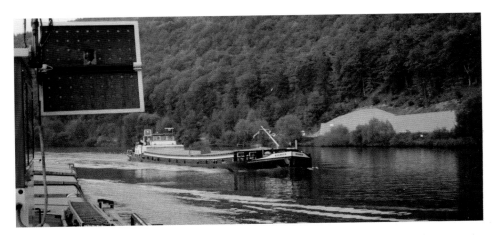

Normal Vessels with a draught of 1m or more must have draught marks permanently inscribed on the hull at maximum 10cm intervals.

If a vessel goes aground or sinks, the Boatmaster must inform the authorities immediately. Someone must stay on board, or nearby, until authorised to leave. If the vessel is a hazard to navigation, warn other vessels in time for them to take avoiding action. Endeavour to clear the channel as quickly as possible.

Protection of the Waterway

It is prohibited to allow any object which could cause damage to project beyond the sides of the vessel.

Anchors when stowed must not project below the bottom of the vessel.

If a potentially hazardous object falls from the vessel, inform the authorities at once and, if possible, mark the spot.

If an unknown obstacle is encountered, inform the authorities at once, detailing its position as accurately as possible.

It is prohibited to tie up to waterway signs or marker buoys, or to damage them in any way. Should damage occur, or be noticed, inform the authorities immediately. The same applies to damage to permanent structures such as locks and bridges, etc.

It is prohibited to throw, or allow to fall, into the water any hazardous substances, particularly petroleum products. In the event of accidental spillage, inform the authorities immediately, specifying the type of spillage and exact location.

Vessels must not be washed, or painted, with prohibited substances.

Household refuse, sewage residues, contaminated bilge water or other special wastes may only be disposed of at appropriate reception facilities. Domestic waste water may only be discharged in accordance with national regulations.

PROHIBITIONS

General no entry/no passage
can be indicated by a sign, red lights, boards or flags

Short-term stoppage

Prolonged stoppage
(e.g. a lock which is out of action)

Three red lights in any configuration at a lock mean it is in use as a weir and craft must keep clear.

Short-term stoppage

Prolonged stoppage
(e.g. a lock which is out of action)

No entry except for non-motorised Small Craft

No overtaking

No overtaking for Convoys over 110m x 12m

No meeting or overtaking *(effectively one-way traffic here)*

No berthing
(i.e. no mooring or anchoring)

No berthing within a lateral distance of (e.g. 40) metres out from sign

No anchoring

No mooring

No turning

Do not make wash

No passage outside the marked area

 or or

No passage, but prepare to get under way
(one of two red lights goes out)

Signs mounted on certain craft

No entry to a port or sidearm

Boarding prohibited

(Rhine areas equivalents)

No smoking or naked flames

Lateral berthing prohibited within (e.g. 25) metres

OTHER TRAFFIC LIGHTS

Two flashing yellow lights signal that a craft is coming out of a port or side arm. Traffic on the main waterway must alter course or speed accordingly. In France, one flashing yellow is also used. One flashing yellow means entry into that same port or sidearm is forbidden. Two yellows signify entry is permitted, but with great caution.

 or (isophase flashing)

Recommendation to steer from the fixed white light towards the isophase flashing one

White lights also give advance warning of difficulty ahead

 or

Stop as required by the regulations

 or

You may proceed

On certain sectors of the Rhine luminous signs advise upstream vessels of the presence and size of any downstream traffic they might meet

One or more convoys over 100m long in the sector | **One or more convoys under 100m long in the sector** | **At least one isolated vessel in the sector** | **No vessels in the sector**

Movable Bridges

 or plus or or

Passage at movable bridges is controlled by red and green lights. If yellow lights show at the same time as one or two reds, passage is permitted for vessels of reduced height appropriate to the bridge clearance shown. One yellow signifies two-way traffic, two yellows signify one-way traffic in your favour (see Passage Through Fixed Bridges – page 39).

+ 0,40

- 0,25

Minimum clearance available (in metres) can be determined by adding or deducting the figure on the pointer to/from the adjacent height gauge.

MANDATORY

Go in direction indicated by the arrow

Channel moves to port

Channel moves to starboard

Keep to port side of channel

Keep to starboard side of channel

Cross channel to port
(this shows you will be meeting other vessels starboard to starboard and should display a blue board – see Rules of the Road)

Cross channel to starboard
(upstream traffic gives priority to downstream traffic during these two crossing manoeuvres)

Stop as necessary

Do not exceed (e.g.12) km/h

Sound your horn

Keep a sharp lookout

Do not enter, or cross, the main waterway if this obliges other vessels to alter course or speed

Make VHF contact on ship-to-ship channel
(normally 10)

Make VHF contact on channel indicated

Normal Vessels are required to have two ATIS-enabled VHF radios; one is ordinarily kept on the ship-to-ship Channel (10) and the other on the local nautical information channel. Belgium applies this to all vessels over 7m. Vessels should announce their presence on the ship-to-ship channel when entering blind sections, narrow channels or bridge openings.

RESTRICTIONS

**Depth
of water
limited**

**Headroom
limited**

**Width of
passage or
channel limited**

**There are restrictions
on navigation – make
enquiries**

**Channel is
(e.g. 40) metres
from the bank**

Transverse current
(to be introduced)

RECOMMENDATIONS

Recommended passage

Two-way traffic

or

One-way traffic

The recommended arch or span through a fixed bridge may be marked by yellow diamonds (or occasionally by yellow lights). If there is a recommended passage, craft use unmarked spans at their own risk.

If there is a recommended span it will always be marked by two yellow diamonds (or lights). If you can see both there will be a 'No Entry' sign on the other side, and it is one-way traffic in your favour. If you can see only one of them then the second is on the other side of the span, allowing traffic in either direction.

or

Recommendation to keep within the space indicated

**Recommendation to follow
direction of the arrow**

GENERAL AUTHORISATION TO PASS
can be indicated by sign, flags, green lights or boards

INDICATIONS

**Entry permitted to
a port or sidearm**

**Overhead
cable**

Weir

**Ferry not
operating
independently**

**Self-propelled
Ferry**

**Berthing
permitted**

**Anchoring
permitted**

**Mooring
permitted**

**Mooring only for
putting vehicles
on or off**

**Berthing
permitted within
a lateral distance
of (e.g. 60)
metres out from
the sign**

**Berthing permitted
within a lateral distance
of between (e.g. 30–60)
metres out from the sign**

**Maximum
number
of vessels
permitted to
berth abreast**

Commercial roadsteads (Rhine areas)

Berthing reserved for various categories of commercial craft (may have additional marking on the white shape)

You are on the major route

Major route ahead

Turning area

End of prohibition or obligation

Drinking water

Telephone

VHF channel in local use

400v electricity point (Rhine areas)

MANY SIGNS MAY HAVE EXPLANATORY OR SUPPLEMENTARY PANELS ATTACHED, FOR EXAMPLE:

Attention Ferry (BAC) ahead

Speed limit 10kph in 1000m

No berthing for 1000m in direction of the arrow

Lateral berthing prohibited within (e.g. 25) metres

Note that if a distance is marked at the top of the sign it signifies something that will happen after that distance; on a pointer to one side it signifies that it starts from the sign and continues for the specified distance; on a pointer below the sign it applies out into the waterway for that distance.

Within CEVNI the left bank or left-hand side is the bank or side on your left as you face downstream, or on a canal downhill through the locks. Left and right banks are a fixed frame of reference, no matter which direction you are actually travelling.

However IALA European buoyage uses red buoys to mark the port side of the channel when coming from the sea, and green buoys to mark the starboard side. As you cross the seaward limit or pass through a lock the buoyage continues using red and green in the same manner as you travel upstream or uphill, i.e. red to port and green to starboard.

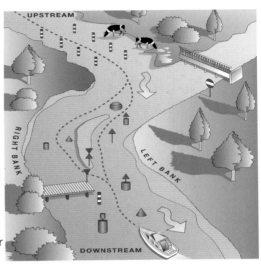

When these two differing frames of reference coincide it means that the red/port buoys are on the 'right hand side' of the waterway – they become the right bank of the channel.

This apparent contradiction can cause difficulty, and it is important not to fall into the trap of thinking of red buoyage as being 'on the left' when travelling upstream. If you always think in terms of port and starboard for buoyage, the left and right banks should be much simpler.

A canal which follows the course of a river is a lateral canal. There are also junction canals which cross from one river valley to another. On these, as you go initially uphill through the locks any red/port buoys will be on your port hand. But then you travel across a summit level and although travelling in the same direction you are now going downhill; the red buoys will now be to starboard. The left and right banks will also change over at this point.

On the summit level itself the authorities will define one particular direction to be regarded as "downhill", which will define how you treat any buoyage you may find, and probably more significantly which craft is to be regarded as travelling downstream under the rules of the road.

Green and red buoys are often found inland used in isolation to steer craft away from a particular obstruction. On channel markers, old buoyage may still be encountered which uses black instead of green.

CHANNEL MARKS

Left-hand side of the channel
Green conical buoys, or buoys/spars with a conical topmark. May have rhythmic green light and radar reflector.

Right-hand side of the channel
Red cylindrical buoys, or buoys/spars with a cylindrical topmark. May have rhythmic red light and radar reflector.

 A white letter 'P' on a green or red buoy means that the channel is next to a berthing area. If it has a light it will flash at a different rhythm to other buoys marking the channel.

Bifurcation of the channel
Red and green horizontal striped spherical buoys, or buoys/spars with a spherical topmark. May have continuous quick, isophase or group flashing (3) white light and radar reflector.

Main channel
The main channel may be indicated by the addition of a green cone or red cylinder with appropriate rhythmic green or red light. Passage is still permitted on either side, but for the main deep water channel they should be regarded as starboard or port buoys as shown by the topmark.

Land Marks

These are marks on top of posts. May have rhythmic green or red lights fitted.

Channel is close to left bank

Channel is close to right bank

Cross-overs

Where the channel crosses from one bank to the other, you will see a post with one of these topmarks:

Left bank marks

May have a yellow flashing or occulting lights with an odd number characteristic (other than 3).

Right bank marks

May have a yellow flashing or occulting lights with an even number characteristic (other than 2).

Simple Cross-over

NOTE: The following topmarks are now being phased out:

Long Cross-overs

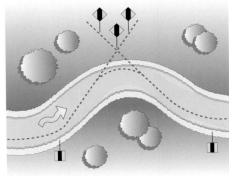

OBSTACLE MARKS

Fixed Marks

Fixed marks are cones or triangular boards on a post. Left-hand marks are green and point up. Right-hand ones are red and point down. They may have rhythmic green or red lights.

Bifurcations are red over green cones/triangles. They may have a continuous, quick isophase, or group flashing (3) white lights.

Bank walls on the approaches to secondary arms and waterways or harbour entrances may be marked as far as the dividing mole by these marks. Vessels entering harbour are regarded as upstream traffic.

Buoyage

Left-hand
Green/white horizontal striped spars or spar buoys with a green cone topmark. They may have rhythmic green lights and generally have a radar reflector. Earlier black and white ones may still be seen.

Right-hand
Red/white horizontal striped spars or spar buoys with a red cylinder topmark. They may have rhythmic red lights and generally have a radar reflector.

ADDITIONAL MARKS FOR NAVIGATION BY RADAR

Bridge Piers

May be marked by yellow floats carrying a radar reflector...

...or by a radar reflector on a pole, upstream and downstream of the piers.

Overhead Cables

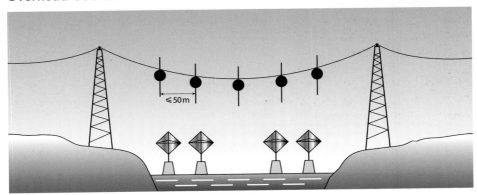

Overhead cables may be marked by radar reflectors attached to the cable at a maximum 50m apart. The radar image will be seen as a series of points to identify the cable.

They may also be marked by radar reflectors on yellow floats, arranged in pairs, near each bank, each giving a radar image of two points side-by-side to identify the cable.

FLOOD MARKS

Certain rivers use flood marks bearing a reference level and a Roman numeral. Some rivers are closed to navigation when level II is reached. On others, such as the Moselle for instance, it is level III.

ADDITIONAL BUOYAGE & MARKS ON LAKES AND BROAD WATERS

Cardinal Marks

The four quadrants North, East, South, and West are bounded by the true bearings NW–NE, NE–SE, SE–SW, SW–NW, taken from the point of interest.

The cardinal mark is named after the quadrant in which it is placed, and indicates that the mark should be passed on the side of the quadrant named.

Lights

Lights, if fitted, are white.

North Cardinal Continuous quick or very quick light.
East Cardinal Group flashing (3) quick or very quick lights.
South Cardinal Group flashing (6) quick or very quick followed by one long light.
West Cardinal Group flashing (9) quick or very quick light.

Isolated Danger Marks

Erected on, or moored above, an isolated danger which has safe water all around it.

May have white group flashing (2) lights.

Safe Water Marks

These mark the axis or middle of a channel, or a landfall.

Lights, if fitted, are white isophase, single-occulting, one long flash/10 secs, or Morse Code A (one short one long).

Weather Warnings on Lakes

Caution warning: A yellow light with about 40 flashes per minute indicates the probable onset of a dangerous phenomenon at an unspecified time.

Danger warning: A yellow light with about 90 flashes per minute indicates the imminent arrival of a dangerous phenomenon.

Restricted Areas

Marked by yellow buoys, possibly with a yellow X topmark. Lights, if fitted, are yellow. Rhythm will be different from that on other foregoing buoyage for lakes. As far as possible, the nature of the restriction or prohibition will be made clear on charts, by markings on the buoy, or by signage on the bank.

A zone where navigation is totally prohibited may be marked by a rigid red pennant on the buoys.

If a prohibited or restricted area is crossed by a channel permitting vessels to pass, the upper half of the two buoys at the entrance may be coloured red on the right-hand side of the entrance and green on the left-hand side, as seen by the Boatmaster leaving the channel.

In France, spherical yellow buoys are generally used to mark an area reserved for bathing. Conical buoys delineate one form of activity from another.

Authorised

Motorised craft

Pleasure craft

Waterskiing

Sailing

Rowing boats and canoes

Windsurfing

High speed boats

Launching

Personal watercraft

Forbidden

Motorised craft

Pleasure craft

Waterskiing

Sailing

Rowing boats and canoes

Windsurfing

High speed boats

Launching

Personal watercraft

Many sound signals are different from those used at sea or on UK inland waterways.

A short blast is about one second, and a long blast four seconds, with about one second between each blast.

A 'series of very short blasts' is six or more quarter-second blasts with about a quarter-second between each blast.

A bell peal is about four seconds, and can also be made by banging two pieces of metal together.

It is prohibited to use signals other than those laid down, and these may only be used as defined.

Sound signals by Convoys will be given by the vessel carrying the Boatmaster.

Normal Vessels have an all-round yellow light synchronised with the horn.

Small Craft are exempt from many of the rules, and give way to Normal Vessels. It follows therefore that there are certain signals they will not use. The helmsman must obviously know the full range in order to be aware of the intentions of other craft, but the ones available to a Small Craft are coloured blue in the following table.

▪	I am steering to (or holding to) starboard
▪ ▪	I am steering to (or holding to) port
▪ ▪ ▪	I am going astern
▪ ▪ ▪ ▪	I am unable to manoeuvre
■ ■ ■ ■ ■	Do not overtake me
▮▮▮▮▮▮	Imminent danger of collision (six or more very short blasts)
▬	Caution
■ ■	I am turning (or turning about) to starboard
■ ■ ■	I am turning (or turning about) to port
■ ■ ■	I wish to overtake on your starboard side
■ ■ ■ ■	I wish to overtake on your port side
■ ■ ■	I am exiting from a port or sidearm and crossing the waterway
■ ■ ■ ■	I am exiting/entering a port or sidearm and turning to starboard
■ ■ ■ ■ ■	I am exiting/entering a port or sidearm and turning to port

DISTRESS SIGNALS

.... Repeated long blasts on the horn or

.... the ringing of a bell = distress signal

The sound signal one short followed by one long blast [■ ▬ ■ ▬] repeated for 15 minutes or more and in conjunction with the synchronised all-round yellow light is the "Do not approach" signal indicating a leakage of dangerous substances. Vessels should take all possible measures to avoid the danger. This signal has a different meaning in the Russian Federation.

In the Netherlands, four short blasts followed by one long signifies "I am in need of medical assistance" and the Morse signal K [▬ ■ ▬] is traditionally used for "Please open the bridge".

SOUND SIGNALS

A vessel (other than a downstream vessel navigating by radar) sounds one long blast once every minute.

Some Authorities may prescribe that a towed convoy or boats abreast under way (other than downstream vessels navigating by radar) sound two long blasts once every minute.

Vessels (other than Small Craft) travelling downstream and navigating under radar sound a series of three ascending tones (e.g. doh-re-mi) three times in succession, with a total length of two seconds. This is repeated as often as necessary.

A Ferry, not navigating by radar.

GENERAL RULES

(Competent authorities may set out other general rules for visibility less than 1 km)

Vessels under way when visibility is reduced owing to fog, haze, snow, rain or other reasons shall navigate by radar, and adjust their speed to suit the conditions and circumstances. A person with appropriate certification must be present in the wheelhouse, with a second person available.

Vessels shall use radio telephone to keep other ships informed of their movements. Small Craft may communicate with the competent authorities instead.

When stopping, vessels must keep clear of the fairway.

Vessels shall generally keep to the starboard side of the fairway, meeting other vessels port to port. Meeting starboard to starboard may be allowed if conditions of certain waterways require it.

Towed Convoys shall not proceed downstream other than to the nearest safe berthing area, nor upstream if there is insufficient visibility between the tug and tow.

STATIONARY VESSELS

Vessels moored, at anchor or aground other than in harbours or designated berthing areas, shall maintain a listening watch on the ship-to-ship channel. If they hear the approach of a vessel they shall sound one peal of a bell if they are on the left-hand side of the fairway, two peals if on the right-hand side, or three peals if their position is uncertain.

NAVIGATION BY RADAR

A vessel travelling upstream which observes an oncoming vessel on the radar screen or which approaches a sector where such vessel may not yet be visible shall announce by radio its category, name, direction and position, and agree a procedure for passing.

A vessel proceeding downstream which observes a vessel which has not yet established contact shall radio the oncoming vessel and agree a procedure for passing. When radio contact cannot be established with the oncoming vessel, a vessel (other than a Small Craft) shall sound a three-tone signal and repeat it as often as necessary (this provision may be waived by authorities or applicable only on certain waterways). The vessel shall reduce speed and stop if necessary.

An upstream vessel, on hearing the three-tone signal, shall sound one long blast, repeated as required. It shall reduce speed and stop if necessary.

Any vessel called by radio shall reply to announce its category, name, direction and position, and agree a procedure for passing. Small Craft shall only indicate the side on which it is giving way.

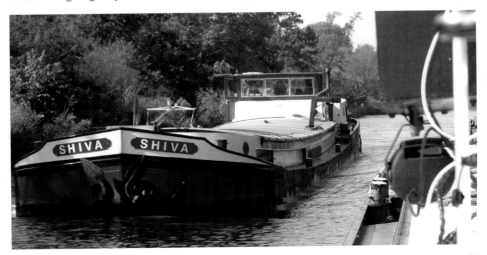

PROVISIONS FOR VESSELS NOT NAVIGATING BY RADAR

Vessels without radar shall proceed immediately to the nearest safe berthing or anchoring areas. During this passage they shall remain as far as possible to the starboard side of the fairway, and should sound one long blast at least once a minute (a convoy may be required to sound two long blasts instead). A lookout must be at the bow, visible from the steering position or in voice contact.

If called by radio by another vessel they must state their category, name, direction, position, and that they are not navigating by radar, and agree a passing procedure.

If such vessel hears the sound signal of another vessel, with which it has not been able to establish radio contact it shall stay as close as possible to the bank, and if necessary stop there until this vessel has passed. If the vessel is not near to a bank, and especially if it is crossing from one bank to the other, it should clear the fairway as soon as possible.

Ferries not navigating by radar shall sound one long blast followed by four short ones, at least once a minute.

AUTOMATIC IDENTIFICATION SYSTEM EQUIPMENT (AIS)

AIS equipment must be of an approved type. All vessels using an AIS device must also be equipped with VHF for ship-to-ship transmission.

RADIO

Radio telephone equipment must be of an approved type and used in accordance with the relevant regulations.

Motor Vessels, other than Small Craft, Ferries and Floating Equipment, should have two radios, one tuned to the navigation information channel and the other to the ship-to-ship channel (Ch10).

Vessels should announce their presence before entering blind sections, narrow channels, or bridge openings. Vessels should state the type of vessel they are, their direction of travel and their position.

DEFINITIONS

For the purpose of CEVNI, waterways are divided into two classes:

CLASS 1 waterways	Normally large rivers
CLASS 2 waterways	Canals, lakes and broad waterways
UPSTREAM	Towards the source of the river, or, on a canal, uphill through the locks. On the summit level of a canal, 'upstream' is determined by the canal authorities.
MEETING	Two vessels travelling on courses directly opposed to each other.
OVERTAKING	A vessel comes from behind another vessel and overtakes it.
CROSSING	Two vessels approaching each other in any manner other than meeting or overtaking.
GIVE-WAY VESSEL	The vessel which, when two vessels are meeting or crossing, must give way to the other.
STAND-ON VESSEL	The vessel which, when two vessels are meeting or crossing, maintains its course and speed.

GENERAL PRINCIPLES

Meeting or overtaking is permitted only when the channel is unquestionably wide enough for safe, simultaneous passage.

Vessels should not change their course or speed in a manner which might lead to danger of collision.

If collision cannot be avoided solely by the action of the give-way vessel, the stand-on vessel must manoeuvre to avoid collision.

LAKES

On lakes, outside of the buoyed channels the steerage rules are the same as those for the prevention of collisions at sea. Apart from certain passenger vessels, Normal Vessels or commercial vessels DO NOT have the absolute priority they enjoy on rivers and canals but must give way to sail and unpowered craft.

SMALL CRAFT

The term 'Small Craft' in this section includes towed Convoys and vessels abreast if comprised wholly of Small Craft.

Small Craft give absolute priority to all other craft, with the exceptions of hydrofoils and hovercraft.

Unless any specific rule states otherwise, Small Craft must give all other craft (except hydrofoils and hovercraft) enough room to hold their course or to manoeuvre.

It follows, therefore, that many of the rules applicable to Normal Vessels do not apply to Small Craft. It is, however, essential that the helmsman of a Small Craft understands what a Normal Vessel is doing.

Small Craft Between Themselves

Crossing and Meeting

A motorised Small Craft gives way to all other Small Craft, and a Small Craft without an engine gives way to a Small Craft under sail.

When two small motorised craft are crossing, the vessel which has the other on its starboard side gives way. However, a Small Craft on the starboard

side of a marked channel should maintain its course.

When two Small Craft under sail are crossing or meeting they follow the rules set out for normal sailing craft.

When two small motorised craft meet and there may be a danger of collision, each steers starboard to pass to port.

Meeting in Narrow Channels

A Small Craft travelling upstream gives way to one travelling downstream.

When upstream is not defined, the stand-on vessel is the Small Craft with no obstacle to starboard or with the outside of a bend to starboard.

However, a motorised Small Craft normally gives way to a Small Craft under sail.

Overtaking

Generally, the Small Craft which is overtaking passes to port of the vessel being overtaken.

If the channel is unquestionably wide enough it may overtake on the starboard side. It shall not oblige the overtaken craft to change its course or speed.

A Small Craft under sail and overtaking another generally passes on the side to which the overtaken vessel has the wind.

A Small Craft being overtaken by a Small Craft under sail should allow it to overtake on the side on which the wind is coming from (the windward side).

Entering and Exiting Ports and Side Arms

Small Craft shall not turn about or exit/enter any port or side arm if such manoeuvre is likely to oblige other vessels, including other Small Craft, to change their course or speed.

High-Speed Vessels

High-Speed Vessels must leave all other vessels room to hold their course and to manoeuvre.

GENERAL RULES

Normal Crossing Rules

When two Normal Vessels are crossing and there is danger of collision, the vessel which has the other to starboard shall give way.

However, a vessel on the starboard side of a marked channel should maintain its course.

The foregoing rule shall not apply if one of the vessels is turning, leaving a berth, or entering/exiting a port or side arm.

It should perhaps be reiterated that all Small Craft, including those under sail, give way to Normal Vessels. Small Craft are defined by size, not by function. A pleasure craft over 20m will therefore be classed as a Normal Vessel along with cargo carriers, passenger boats and other working craft.

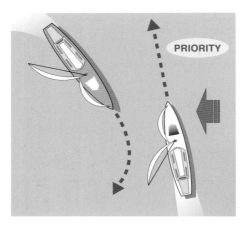

When two vessels under sail are crossing, the vessel with the wind on its starboard side has priority.

If they both have the wind on the same side, the give-way vessel is the one to windward.

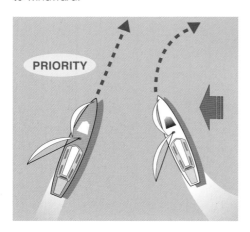

If a vessel with the wind to port cannot determine whether the crossing vessel has the wind to port or starboard, it shall give way.

A frequent complaint of commercial skippers is the general lack of understanding by pleasure boaters of 'blue boarding'. There is no real equivalent within the COLREGS applicable at sea, where passing starboard-to-starboard is only legitimate to 'avoid immediate danger'.

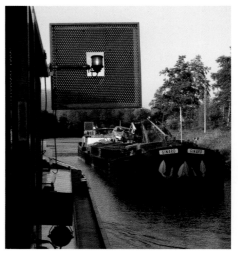

The manoeuvre may be carried out by choice, ordinarily prompted by the vessel travelling upstream. A vessel travelling up against the current may decide to keep to the port side of the fairway if the flow is less strong. This puts him on the 'wrong' side should he meet a vessel coming downstream. The rules say he should not impede the passage of the downstream vessel, and he may therefore opt to show that he is allowing the oncoming vessel an appropriate passage to starboard instead of to port. It is also permissible in very rare instances for certain downstream vessels to indicate they wish to pass starboard-to-starboard. These departures from normal rules are not available to Small Craft in relation to another vessel or other small craft, nor between two high-speed vessels or a high-speed vessel and any other craft.

The manoeuvre may also be mandatory by signs B4 and B3a (see p.36). One fairly common instance is where it keeps a downstream vessel out of the weir stream as it comes to a lock. The rules do not demand a blue board to be shown, but it is generally done for avoidance of doubt – showing that the signage has been seen and understood.

There is nothing requiring a Small Craft to carry a blue board or flag and they may give the appropriate sound signals instead. However, it is preferable to have something blue, especially for a craft that is borderline length and has a barge shape, again for avoidance of doubt. A Normal Vessel's board/flag should be 1m square, 0.60m for a Small Craft.

Normal Meeting Rules

Normal Vessels travelling upstream give way to those travelling downstream.

If the upstream vessel wants the downstream vessel to pass port to port as normal, he gives no signal.

If he wishes to leave the downstream vessel a course to pass starboard to starboard, he displays on his starboard side, by day, a bright scintillating white light, and/or a blue board, or a blue flag. By night, he displays a scintillating white light, and possibly also a blue board.

If the upstream vessel thinks that the downstream vessel has not understood his intentions, he will give one short blast if he is leaving a passage to port, and two short blasts if he is leaving a passage to starboard.

Downhill vessels shall take the course indicated by the upstream vessel, and repeat the visual or sound signals made by the upstream vessel.

For simplicity the term 'blue board' has been used to include the various visual signals. The terms 'upstream vessel' and 'downstream vessel' refer here to a vessel travelling upstream or travelling downstream respectively.

The Pusher (A) travelling upstream is 'blue-boarding' the Barge (B) travelling downstream in the middle. The Barge acknowledges this and they pass starboard-to-starboard. The Barge (C) shows no signal as he is passing in the normal way, port-to-port. The Small Craft (D) simply keeps out of the way.

These signals will be retracted after the meeting unless it is necessary to continue passing vessels to starboard.

However, if a passenger vessel travelling downstream wants to call at a landing stage on the side used by the upstream vessel, or a towed Convoy moving downstream wants to keep close to a particular bank, it has the right to ask the upstream vessel to change course using the sound signals as described above.

If the upstream vessel sees that the course requested by the downstream one will cause danger of collision it will sound a series of very short blasts. The helmsman will then take all necessary steps to avoid the danger.

When two vessels meet and there is any risk of collision each shall veer to starboard, thus passing port-to-port. However, if both vessels are under sail, the rules regarding Sailing Vessels apply.

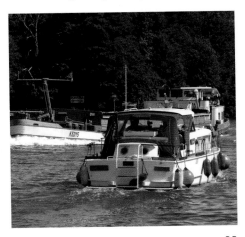

Meeting Vessels Towed from the Bank

If a vessel meets another being towed from the bank, it passes on the side away from the towline.

Meeting in Narrow Channels

On waterways where 'upstream' and 'downstream' are defined, if an upstream vessel sees a downstream vessel approaching a narrow channel, it shall stop and wait until the downstream vessel has passed.

A downstream vessel which can see that an upstream vessel has already entered the narrow channel shall stop above the channel until the vessel has passed.

When 'upstream' and 'downstream' are not defined, the Normal Vessel with no obstacle to starboard, or with the outside of a bend to starboard, shall hold its course and other vessels should wait until it has passed. If two Normal Sailing Vessels or two Small Craft under sail meet, the vessel to windward, or, if both are navigating with the wind, the vessel with the wind on its starboard side maintains its course, and the other vessel waits until it has cleared the narrow channel.

If there is a restricted view of the channel, a vessel shall sound one long blast before entering, and as often as necessary while proceeding.

When meeting in a narrow channel is inevitable, vessels shall ensure they pass at a point, and in a manner, to minimise

danger. If there is danger of collision a series of very short blasts should be sounded.

Meeting Prohibited by Signs

A4

Where meeting is prohibited by sign A4 the rules for meeting in narrow channels apply.

Where a one-way traffic system is in force, prohibition of passage is indicated by signs A1, and authorisation by signs E1.

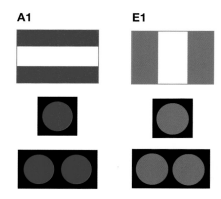

A1   **E1**

Overtaking

Overtaking is permitted only if it can be carried out without danger. The overtaken vessel shall slow down if necessary to make the procedure quick and safe.

Vessels will generally overtake on the port side of the overtaken vessel, but can do so to starboard if the channel is sufficiently wide.

If the overtaken vessel is required to alter course, or it appears not to have noticed the overtaking vessel, the overtaking vessel sounds two long blasts followed by two short blasts to pass to port, and two long blasts followed by one short blast to pass to starboard.

If the overtaken vessel agrees to this, it sounds one short blast to be overtaken to port, and two short blasts to be overtaken to starboard.

If overtaking is not possible on the side requested, the overtaken vessel sounds one short blast if it is possible to overtake to port, and two short blasts if it is possible to overtake to starboard.

The overtaking vessel then sounds one or two short blasts as appropriate to signal its change of direction.

When overtaking cannot be carried out without danger, the vessel to be overtaken sounds five short blasts.

An overtaking vessel under sail shall generally pass on the side on which the overtaken vessel has the wind. The overtaken vessel should facilitate this.

Small Craft may not overtake if it requires the overtaken vessel to change its course or speed.

(A) The motor barge sounds two long and two short blasts to signal he wishes to overtake to port of the pusher. Two long mean "I wish to overtake", and two short mean "I am steering to port."

(B) The pusher replies with two short blasts, saying this is not possible (effectively saying "I am steering to port") with the consequence that the give-way vessel behind him cannot then come through on that side.

(C) The motor barge then sounds one short blast to signal he wishes to overtake to starboard instead. The pusher will not now give any further signal unless there is any doubt about what is happening.

Overtaking is prohibited generally on sections marked by the sign A2 or A4. Overtaking between Convoys (where at least one is pushed and >110m x 12m) is prohibited on sections marked by A3.

A2   **A3**   **A4**

On the Rhône, a vessel displays a blue flag at the bow (or all-round white light at night) when overtaking.

Sections with a Prescribed Course

These are marked by signs B1, B2, B3 or B4.

B1

B2   **B3**   **B4**

B3a   **B3b**   **B4b**

Vessels travelling upstream shall in no circumstances impede the progress of downstream vessels whilst manoeuvring in accordance with these signs.

Turning and Leaving or Joining a Waterway

Turning, leaving berths or anchorages, or entering/exiting harbours and side arms can only be carried out without obliging other vessels to make abrupt changes to course or speed.

Turning

A vessel which requires other vessels to alter course or speed so it can turn, sounds one long blast, followed by one short, to signal turning to starboard, or two short to signal turning to port. Other vessels shall then facilitate the turn, particularly when the turning vessel needs to turn up to head up into the current.

Turning at approved turning places is bound by these same rules.

Vessels Leaving a Berth or Anchorage

A vessel which requires other vessels to alter course or speed so it can leave a berth or anchorage sounds one short blast when vessels are approaching on its starboard side, and two short blasts when vessels are approaching on its port side.

Approaching vessels shall then facilitate the departure.

Entering and Exiting Harbours and Side Arms

A downstream vessel wanting to turn upstream to enter a harbour or side arm must give priority to an upstream vessel which also wishes to enter the same harbour or side arm.

If it requires other vessels to alter course or speed, the manoeuvring vessel, when entering or leaving, shall sound three long blasts, followed by one short if turning to starboard, or followed by two short if turning to port.

If after leaving it wishes to cross the waterway it sounds three long blasts. Before completing the crossing, it then sounds one long followed by one short to turn to starboard, or one long followed by two short to turn to port.

ENTERING AND EXITING PORTS AND SIDE ARMS
Vessel (A) travelling upstream signals three long blasts and two short to indicate he is turning into the side arm.
Vessel (B) coming downstream also wishes to enter this arm. Vessel (B) must give priority to Vessel (A) before he signals to say he is turning about. He too will then give the three long/two short signal as he is about to enter the arm.

Vessel (A) signals three long blasts and two short to indicate he is turning into the side arm.
Vessel (B) sounds two short blasts to say he is moving to port, out of the way.
Vessel (C) sounds three long blasts to say he is entering the main waterway and crossing it. He then sounds one long blast and one short to indicate he is turning to starboard. Two flashing yellow lights at the entrance also warn craft of his entry into the main waterway.

Other vessels modify their course and speed as necessary, whether or not the harbour/side arm is controlled by yellow flashing lights.

If the signs below are used, vessels may not leave the harbour/side arm if Normal Vessels on the main waterway would need to modify their course or speed.

Exit from a harbour/side arm may be controlled by red and green traffic lights. If passage is permitted by the appropriate green signal, other vessels modify their course or speed to facilitate this.

Other Steerage Rules

Vessels may travel abreast only if there is sufficient room to do so in safety.

Except when overtaking or meeting, it is prohibited to navigate within 50m of vessels displaying two or three blue cones by day (or two or three all-round blue lights at night).

In France, this is one or two red cones by day, one all-round red or two alternating flashing red lights at night.

It is prohibited to go alongside a vessel under way without permission of its Boatmaster.

Trailing anchors, cables or chains is prohibited.

Drifting is prohibited.

Vessels must regulate their speed and not create excessive wash likely to cause damage to other vessels or structures.

When encountering any of the general 'no passage' signs (see p.8) vessels must stop short of the sign.

PASSAGE THROUGH BRIDGES

Unless there is sufficient width for simultaneous passage of two or more vessels, the rules for passage of narrow channels apply (see p.34).

Passage may be marked by signs A10 prohibiting navigation outside of the area between the two signs, or D2 recommending that vessels remain within the area between the two signs.

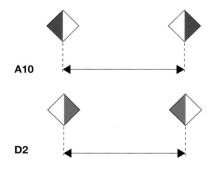

A10

D2

Fixed Bridges

Prohibited spans of fixed bridges may be marked by no entry signs or lights A1 (see p.34).

Other spans may be marked by yellow diamonds to signify they are the preferred openings. One yellow diamond signifies it is open to traffic in each direction. Two yellow diamonds indicate that it is closed to traffic from the other direction.

Unmarked openings may be used at the Boatmaster's own risk.

Movable Bridges

Obey any instructions given by bridge staff.

Slow down on approach.

If you cannot or do not wish to proceed, stop short of any 'stop' sign.

Overtaking on the approach is prohibited.

Passage may be regulated by traffic lights:

- One or more reds signify passage prohibited.

- Red and green in conjunction alert vessels to be prepared to pass.

- One or more green signal that passage is permitted.

Two red lights, one over the other, signify that navigation is suspended. However,

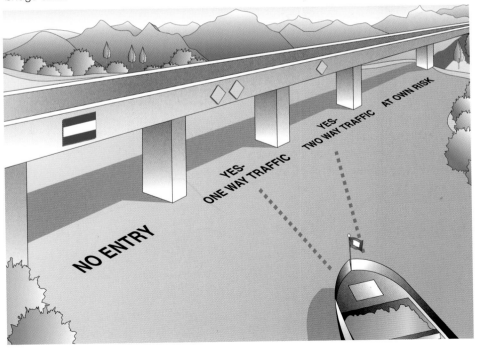

a yellow light in conjunction with one or two reds allows passage by vessels of restricted airdraught (one yellow signifies passage in each direction, and two signify passage prohibited in the other direction).

Red, green, or yellow boards may be used instead of lights.

WEIRS

Trailing of anchors, cables or chains near a weir is prohibited.

Passage through an opening in a weir is permitted where you see green signs E1.

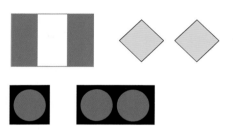

Passage is prohibited if any general red signs A1 are displayed, except that vessels with sufficiently low airdraught may proceed if yellow sign D1 shows on an overhead bridge.

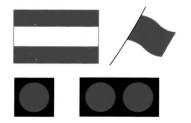

PASSAGE THROUGH LOCKS

A vessel must slow down when arriving at a lock. If it cannot, or does not wish to proceed, it must stop short of any 'stop' sign. Overtaking in lock approaches is prohibited.

Boatmasters must communicate by VHF on the channel assigned to the lock.

Passage through a lock is in order of arrival. However, Small Craft are not entitled to a separate locking. They must wait until they are asked to enter by the lock staff. If locking through with Normal Vessels, Small Craft must enter the lock last, and keep clear of the Normal Vessels.

However, certain vessels have priority of passage, and fly a long red pennant at the bow to signify this. They will generally be vessels of the navigation authority, fire, police, customs etc., or passenger boats on a public service. France also allows priority to tugs without a Convoy, and sea-going ships.

In a Lock

- Anchors must be fully raised.

- Vessels must avoid knocking against any part of the lock or other vessels.

- Vessels must keep within any limits marked on the lock walls.

- Vessels shall be made fast until allowed to leave.

- Fenders are mandatory, and must be floating ones if movable.

- Vessels must not discharge water onto the copings or other vessels.

- Unless otherwise permitted, use of the engine is prohibited from the time the vessel is made fast until it leaves the lock.

It is obligatory to keep at least 10m from a vessel carrying inflammable materials (displaying a blue cone or light). These vessels will not be locked through at the same time as a passenger vessel.

Vessels carrying two or three blue cones/lights (one or two reds in France) are locked separately.

To ensure safe and orderly navigation, lock staff may give instructions which vary from these provisions. All vessels must comply with such instruction.

Visual Signals

Entering and leaving locks is regulated by visual signals:

- Red and white boards A1 or red lights signify 'entry/exit prohibited'.

- Two red lights one above the other signify 'lock out of service'.

- Green in conjunction with red, or one of a pair of reds becoming extinguished signify 'prepare to enter'.

- Green and white boards E1 or green lights signify 'entry/exit permitted'.

- In the absence of lights/boards, entry/exit is prohibited unless permitted by lock staff.

- Any configuration of three red lights indicates a lock in use as a weir, and craft must keep clear.

Radar-activated locks may have an amber light which indicates the helmsman's telecommand has been registered. Some locks now have flashing amber lights when gates open and close.

In France, where the smaller Freycinet locks are often automatic and boater-operated, lock failure can be caused by two or more Small Craft working through together.

As the first boat enters the chamber, the control light goes to red. Any subsequent craft is then entering against a red light, leading to complications of the operating electronics. To compound the problem, Small Craft frequently enter the lock with a gap between each craft, but leave bunched up together. This means the electronics register a lesser number of craft leaving. No other craft can then use the lock until maintenance staff sort out the problem!

Berthing

A vessel is berthed when it is directly or indirectly moored to the bank, or at anchor.

A vessel should berth as close to the bank as possible and not obstruct navigation in any way.

Vessels should be berthed to allow for changes in water level and wind, and the suction and wash of passing vessels.

Vessels must not use trees, railings, posts, metal steps and handrails, etc. for making fast or warping.

Berthing is prohibited within:

- 10m of a vessel carrying one blue cone/light.

- 50m of a vessel carrying two blue cones/lights (two red cones, two alternating flashing all-round red lights in France).

- 100m of a vessel carrying three blue cones/lights (one red cone/all-round red light in France).

A vessel berthed in the channel (or a vessel carrying dangerous substances berthed at any place) must maintain a permanent watch on board.

SUR 50 METRES

PROMENEURS, PECHEURS,
A PARTIR DE CE POINT ET SUR UNE DISTANCE DE 50 M.
IL EST INTERDIT DE S'ARRETER

AREAS WHERE BERTHING IS PROHIBITED

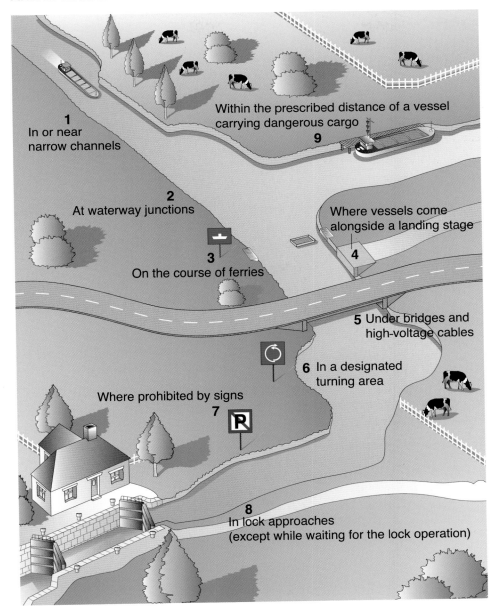

1 In or near narrow channels

Within the prescribed distance of a vessel carrying dangerous cargo
9

2 At waterway junctions

Where vessels come alongside a landing stage

3 On the course of ferries

4

5 Under bridges and high-voltage cables

6 In a designated turning area

Where prohibited by signs
7

8 In lock approaches (except while waiting for the lock operation)

LIGHTS

Masthead Light
Strong white light projecting an uninterrupted beam forward through 225° to 22° 30' abaft the beam.

Side Lights
Bright green to starboard and bright red to port projecting an uninterrupted beam through 112° 30' to 22° 30' abaft the beam.

Stern Light
Ordinary or bright white light projecting an uninterrupted beam aft through 135° to 22° 30' abaft the beam on both sides.

All-round Light
Light projecting an uninterrupted beam through 360°.

Lights prescribed for use at night are to be used in all conditions of poor visibility.

Masthead lights may be carried at a reduced height for passage through bridges, weirs and locks.

VESSELS UNDER WAY

(except when carrying dangerous cargo)

A Single Motorised Normal Vessel
This shows no day marks.* At night it carries a white masthead light, side lights which are below and behind the masthead, and a stern light.

It may carry a second masthead light, higher than and aft of the first. This is mandatory on vessels over 110m.

In Belgium, all vessels under way must fly a red flag with a white square in the centre on a mast.

Motorised Small Craft

At night, a motorised Small Craft shows the same lights as a single Normal Vessel, but bright rather than strong. Side lights may be ordinary.

The side lights may be together in one lamp. The masthead and stern lights may similarly be together in one lamp, at the mast – effectively an all-round white.

The above applies also to Small Craft towing or abreast of other Small Craft. When in tow, or abreast of a Normal Vessel (other than as a tender) a Small Craft carries an all-round white light.

Motorised Small Craft under 7m require only an all-round white light.

Sailing Vessel

At night, a Sailing Vessel shows side lights and stern light only. It may in addition carry at its mast an all-round red over an all-round green.

A Small Craft under sail may use side and stern lights in a sectored lamp at the top of the mast.

A sailing craft under 7m only needs an all-round white light, but should display a second white light upon the approach of another vessel.

If motor-sailing by day it shows, as high as possible, a black cone pointing down, and by night the same lights as an isolated motor vessel of the same size.

Small Craft neither Motorised nor Under Sail

Proceeding alone, this Small Craft should display an all-round white light. A ship's tender only displays this light upon the approach of another vessel.

A Motorised Vessel Leading a Towed Convoy

By day, a Motorised Vessel leading a towed Convoy, or acting as an auxiliary for another Motorised Vessel, displays a yellow cylinder with black and white stripes at each end. If more than one vessel leads the Convoy, each vessel carries the cylinder.

By night, such vessels show two masthead lights, one above the other, and side lights. Its stern light is yellow. If more than one vessel leads the Convoy, each carries three masthead lights.

Vessels under Tow other than Small Craft

By day, vessels under tow display a yellow ball, and by night an all-round white light. The last vessel in the Convoy also shows a white stern light.

If any section of the Convoy is over 110m long, it carries two all-round white lights, one at each end.

If the rearmost section comprises two or more craft abreast, only the two outside vessels carry white stern lights. If the rearmost craft are Small Craft they are discounted in this context.

A Motorised Vessel under way, and temporarily preceded by an auxiliary motor vessel, displays a yellow ball by day. At night, it shows the lights of a single motor vessel under way.

Ships under tow display a yellow ball by day, but may show their side lights instead of an all-round white at night.

Pushed Convoys

A pushed Convoy carries three masthead lights on the bow of the leading vessel (on pushed vessels abreast, the vessel on the port side carries three masthead lights), arranged in a triangle with the point uppermost.

Any other vessel whose full width is visible from ahead carries a white masthead light, lower than the triangle of lights.

Side lights are shown at the widest part of the Convoy, as near to the pusher as possible.

The pusher itself displays three white stern lights in a horizontal line, and every vessel whose full width is visible from the stern shows a white stern light.

If more than two pushed vessels are so visible, only the two outside ones show the stern light.

If the Convoy is preceded at night by one or more auxiliary vessels, the stern lights of the pusher will be yellow. By day, the pusher carries a yellow ball.

If a Convoy is pushed by two pushers abreast, the one providing the main propulsion carries three stern lights, but the other only carries one.

Pushers up to 110m x 12m are considered to be a single motor vessel (92m x 9.5m in France).

Side-by-side Formations

Vessels travelling abreast each show the usual navigation lights, except that the side lights will only be shown at the outside of the formation.

If one of the vessels is unpowered, it shows an all-round light at the mast instead of a sectored one. If preceded by an auxiliary Motorised Vessel they show the same lights, but by day show a yellow ball.

Passenger Vessels

By day, passenger vessels under 20m licensed to carry more than 12 passengers display a yellow bicone visible from all directions (in Belgium, a yellow all-round light at night).

High-Speed Vessels

These carry 2 all-round yellow quick-scintillating lights, by night and by day.

Ferries

Ferries not Moving Independently

These show a green ball visible from all directions by day and an all-round green light over an all-round white at night.

Lead Boat of a Longitudinal-cable Ferry

This displays at night an all-round white light visible from all directions.

Ferries Moving Independently

These show a green ball by day. By night they show an all-round green light over an all-round white, plus the side and stern lights of a Normal Vessel.

Ferries Moving Independently and Enjoying Priority

These show additionally by day a white cylinder below the green ball. Additionally, at night, they show a second all-round green light above the first.

Vessels Enjoying Priority of Passage

When at specified places these show a red pennant at the bow in addition to any other prescribed marks.

Floating Installations and Assemblies of Floating Materials

When under way at night these show sufficient all-round white lights to define their shape and size.

Vessels Unable to Manoeuvre

By day, a red flag may be swung from side to side, or two black balls are shown, visible all round, one above the other. By night, it shows two all-round red lights one above the other, or a red light swung from side to side.

A Small Craft may use a swung white light instead.

Craft will also give the sound signal four short blasts as required.

Vessels with Limited Ability to Manoeuvre

When carrying out works such as cable laying, etc., these will show in addition to other prescribed markings (e.g. navigation lights):

- By night, three all-round lights, i.e. an all-round red over an all-round white over an all-round red.
- By day, a black ball over a black bicone over a black ball.

If their operations cause obstruction they shall additionally show:

- By night, two all-round red lights, one above the other on the side(s) where the obstruction occurs, and two all-round green lights, one above the other, on the side(s) where the channel is clear.
- By day, two black balls one above the other on the side(s) where the obstruction occurs, and two black bicones one above the other on the side(s) where the channel is clear.

These provisions do not apply to Floating Equipment at work when stationary.

Vessels Carrying Dangerous Cargo

By day, vessels carrying dangerous cargo show one, two or three blue cones, pointing downwards and high enough to be visible.

By night, they show one, two or three all-round blue lights. These cones and lights are additional to any other marks or lights prescribed for the category of craft, e.g. the masthead, side and stern light of a Normal Vessel.

- Vessels carrying inflammable materials are defined by one blue cone/light.
- Vessels carrying materials constituting a health hazard are defined by two blue cones/lights.
- Vessels carrying explosives are defined by three blue cones/lights.

If dangerous cargo is carried by a pusher unit it is the pusher that displays the cones/lights, or the Motorised Vessel of a side-by-side formation. If there are two pushers the shapes/lights are shown by the starboard pusher.

These cones and lights continue to be shown when a craft carrying dangerous cargo is moored or at anchor. They are then in addition to the various lights and shapes for each particular type of Stationary Vessel.

Sea-going ships operating temporarily on inland waters may instead display an all-round red light by night and a red swallowtail pennant (code flag B) by day.

In France, the two blue cones/lights are replaced in the day by two red cones and at night by two alternating flashing all-round red lights. The three blue cones/lights are replaced by one red cone/light. In the case of pushed or towed Convoys each vessel shows the appropriate lights/cones.

STATIONARY VESSELS

Vessels carrying dangerous cargo continue additionally to display the appropriate shapes or lights.

Vessel Moored to the Bank

At night, vessels moored directly or indirectly to the bank show an all-round white light on the side nearest to the channel. Vessels may be exempt from this requirement if it is obviously not necessary.

Craft may show two all-round whites, one at the bow and one at the stern, on the side nearest to the channel.

A Vessel Stationary Offshore (at Anchor)

A vessel stationary offshore without direct or indirect access to the bank shows a black ball, visible all-round by day. At night it shows two all-round whites, one at the bow and a lower one at the stern.

A Pushed Convoy Stationary Offshore

By day, a pushed Convoy stationary offshore shows a black ball, visible all-round on the pusher and on the leading vessel or outermost leading vessels of the Convoy. By night, it shows an all-round white on each vessel of the Convoy, with a maximum requirement of four such lights, providing the outline of the Convoy is clearly defined.

Small Craft

Small Craft show an all-round white light in any suitable position.

Ferries not Moving Independently

When moored at their landing stage by night these show an all-round green light over an all-round white. The lead boat of a longitudinal-cable Ferry carries an all-round white light visible from all directions.

Ferries Moving Independently

When moored at their landing stage by night they show an all-round green light over an all-round white. When they cease operation they extinguish the green all-round light.

The key difference between a self-propelled ferry and one not moving independently is that the former has greater manoeuvrability, and is just another boat when it is out of service. A chain or cable ferry does not have the same manoeuvrability, and its chain or cable remains a potential hazard at all times. The lights and shapes reflect this.

Floating Installations and Assemblies of Floating Material

When stationary at night, these show sufficient all-round white lights to define their shape and size.

Floating Equipment at Work, and Grounded or Sunken Vessels

The only vessels which may be protected against wash are seriously damaged vessels, those engaged in rescue work, unable to manoeuvre, or specifically authorised by the authorities. The red over white boards authorising passage with no wash must not be confused with the red/white/red 'passage forbidden' ones.

- On the side(s) on which the channel is clear, by day, two green bicones are shown one above the other, visible all-round, replaced at night by two all-round green lights.
- On the side on which the channel is not clear, by day, a red ball visible all-round, replaced at night by an all-round red light.

- The day symbols may be replaced by the general green/white 'passage permitted' and red/white 'no passage' boards.

Vessels Protected against Wash

- On the side(s) on which the channel is clear, by day a red flag over a white one, or one flag with a red upper half and white lower is shown. These are replaced at night by one all-round red light over one all-round white.
- On the side on which the channel is not clear, by day a red ball visible all round is shown, replaced at night by an all-round red light.

- The day symbols may be replaced by boards with the same colour characteristics.

BALLS AND BICONES

These day marks are used to signify what a vessel is doing, and the safe passage for other craft. The safe passage(s) will be marked with bicones – **you can go by the bicones, but keep clear of the balls**.

A Single Black Ball, or Two Individual Black Balls

These signify respectively a vessel or a convoy at anchor.

Two Black Balls, One above the Other

This is a vessel unable to manoeuvre.

Two Black Balls, One above the Other and Separated by a Black Bicone

This is a vessel unable to manoeuvre by the nature of the works it is carrying out. If this vessel causes obstruction to navigation it will **also show two black balls** on the side forbidden to other craft, and **two black bicones** on the side where passage is permitted.

Coloured Balls and Bicones

Vessels engaged in work that means they are stationary, and grounded or sunk vessels, will not show the 'unable to manoeuvre' ball/bicone/ball, but do use balls and bicones to identify the side other vessels may pass. If there is no obstruction they will show two bicones on each side. It is slightly contradictory, but where the shapes used by a vessel which

is capable of (limited) navigation are black, these vessels which are stationary show **balls and bicones which are red and green**. These will not of course have any relationship with port or starboard.

Three Black Balls in a Triangle

These signify a vessel engaged in minesweeping. Other craft should keep 1km clear of the stern of such vessels.

Two Black Cones, Point to Point

This is a shape unique to trawlers. Other vessels should not pass close to the stern. There will also be a **black cone, point up**, if their trawl exceeds 150m to one side.

A Black Cone, Point Down

This is also used to denote a vessel which is motorsailing.

Blue Cones (or Red, in France)

These denote carriage of dangerous cargo.

Yellow Balls

On a mast, these depict a vessel under tow.

Yellow Bicones on a Mast

These denote a small passenger vessel, with the implication that it might not behave quite as predictably as you may imagine.

Yellow Bicones in the Water

These are marking either an anchor or fishing nets.

Anchors Presenting a Danger to Navigation

Vessels and assemblies of Floating Material, or Floating Installations whose anchors may cause danger to navigation, at night replace the all-round white light nearest to the anchor with two all-round white lights, one above the other. The anchor itself is marked by an all-round white light and radar reflector. By day, the anchor is marked by a yellow float with a radar reflector.

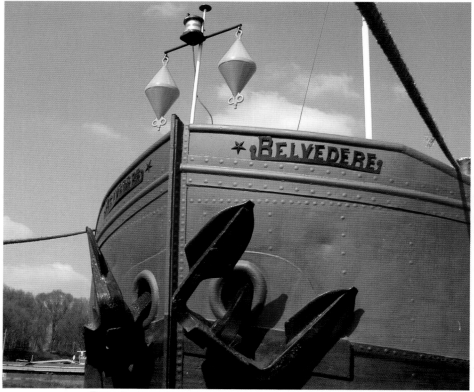

These floats are sometimes seen hung at the bow ready for use.

VESSELS ON SPECIAL ACTIVITY

Fishing Vessels

When stationary, with nets or poles extending into or near the channel, the nets/poles are marked by day with yellow floats sufficient to show their position. By night, the yellow floats are replaced by all-round white lights.

- In addition to other relevant marks, a trawler when working displays, by night, two all-round lights, green over white. The green light is lower than the masthead light and the white light higher than the side lights. A trawler under 50m does not require a masthead light. By day, a trawler displays two black cones, one above the other, point to point.

- Other fishing boats show these same lights and shapes, except that the all-round green is replaced by all-round red, and any masthead light is extinguished.

If fishing boats have tackle extending more than 150m horizontally from the side of the vessel, they additionally display on the tackle side, by day, a black cone pointed upwards and, by night, an all-round white light lower than the other all-round white light but higher than the side lights.

Vessels Engaged in Minesweeping

In addition to other relevant marks, a vessel engaged in minesweeping shows by night three all-round green lights in a triangle, point upwards on the topmast. By day, these are replaced by three black balls in a similar pattern.

Fire Fighting and other Official Vessels

These may show, in addition to other relevant symbols, an all-round scintillating blue light by night and by day. Some authorities may specify yellow instead.

Vessels Carrying out Work and Under Way

These show in addition to other relevant symbols an all-round scintillating yellow light, by night and day.

Vessels used for Diving

These show a rigid reproduction of Code flag A. They may show the various signals for a vessel unable to manoeuvre.

Other vessels shall keep at least 50m (or such other distance as determined) from vessels engaged in diving. Sports diving shall not be practised on the route of a Ferry, at harbour entrances or areas reserved for waterskiing.

In France a red flag with a white diagonal line or white diagonal cross may sometimes be used.

Pilot Vessels

At night, instead of an ordinary masthead light, these shall show two all-round lights one above the other, white over red. They may by day display a blue or red flag, bearing the letter L or P, according to country.

DISTRESS SIGNALS

In addition to, or instead of, the various relevant sound signals the following visual distress signals may be used:

- A flag or other suitable object waved in a circle
- A light waved in a circle
- A flag having above it or below it a ball or similar shape
- Rockets or shells throwing red stars fired into the air
- Red flare
- Flames from burning tar, oil etc.
- A flashed light signal SOS in Morse Code ■■■ ■■ ■■ ■■ ■■■
- Slow repeated up-and-down movements of the arms to each side.

ABOUT THE AUTHOR

Tam Murrell has been boating for business and pleasure since the late 1950s. As owner and operator of commercial vessels ranging from working narrowboats and barges on UK inland waters to small coasters trading in and around the Thames estuary and into northern Europe he has a wide experience of handling craft in a variety of contexts. Since 1995 he and Di, his wife, have spent much of their time on continental waterways on their 24m Dutch barge, and run a barge-handling school in France for RYA and French qualifications.

For your CEVNI test you may be asked a number of questions similar to the following samples.

One of these need not be carried on board:

    a. Boat Certificate of Registry
    b. Navigation Regulations
    c. Credit cards
    d. VHF Licence

On a vessel this means:

    a. I have a diver down
    b. Under 20m carrying more than 12 passengers
    c. Restricted in ability to manoeuvre
    d. Constrained by draught

On a vessel pushing this means:

    a. Fishing
    b. Pilot on board
    c. Not under command
    d. Carrying inflammable materials

A vessel showing this means:

    a. I wish to communicate with you
    b. Vessel enjoying priority of passage
    c. I require medical assistance
    d. I have a diver down

An upstream vessel showing this means:

    a. I am stopping
    b. I am going astern
    c. I am leaving a course for downstream vessels to starboard
    d. Stop

This shape signifies:

    a. A pilot vessel
    b. Towing
    c. Fishing
    d. A ferry

What are the meanings of these signs?

a. No entry
b. Barge ahead
c. Keep a sharp lookout
d. Sound your horn

a. Enter
b. Do not enter
c. Enter with caution
d. Keep a sharp lookout

a. Sign on right-hand bank – cross over to left
b. Sign on left-hand bank – cross over to right
c. Keep in centre of channel
d. No mooring

a. Customs
b. Harbour Office
c. No anchoring
d. Lock

a. You must berth within 500m of the sign
b. No berthing in direction of arrow for 500m
c. Berths for 500 vessels
d. Width of channel 500cm

a. No entry
b. Channel close to left bank
c. Channel close to right bank
d. Channel in centre

This vessel is:

a. Over 110m
b. A crane barge at work
c. A pusher Convoy
d. Wishing to meet starboard to starboard

This sound signal means:

a. Turning to starboard
b. Turning to port
c. Imminent danger of collision
d. Astern propulsion

This vessel is:

a. Not under command
b. Restricted in ability to manoeuvre
c. A Motorised Vessel leading a towed Convoy
d. Constrained by draught

This vessel is:

a. A fuel barge
b. Towing
c. A passenger vessel under 20m
d. A High Speed Vessel

This shape means:

a. Authorised passage ahead
b. Channel close to left bank
c. Channel close to right bank
d. Scenic mooring berth

a. Windsurfing permitted
b. Windsurfing forbidden
c. Recreation area
d. Permission required to windsurf

a. Keep to port
b. Keep to starboard
c. No entry except for non-motorised Small Craft
d. Moorings ahead

a. No power vessels
b. Disengage propeller
c. Authorised passage for motorised craft within this channel
d. Keep a lookout for power vessels

a. Stop as necessary
b. Keep a sharp lookout
c. Low bridge
d. Go astern

a. Overtake here
b. No overtaking
c. Use both sides of channel
d. No entry

a. Berthing permitted
b. Authorised passage
c. Channel close to left bank
d. Keep a sharp lookout

a. Strong current
b. Bends in river
c. Do not create wash which could damage banks and structures
d. No mooring

a. Do not enter
b. Recommended passage, one-way traffic in this direction
c. No mooring
d. Request permission before entering this area

a. Channel moves to port
b. Priority to upstream traffic
c. Beware junction ahead
d. Cross channel to port

This buoy:

a. Marks left-hand side of channel
b. Marks right-hand side of channel
c. Marks a bifurcation of the channel
d. Is a mooring buoy

A Small Craft as opposed to a Normal Vessel is:
a. Under 10m in length
b. Under 13.7m in length
c. Under 20m in length
d. Under 80 tonnes

The meaning of this signal is:

a. A vessel under sail
b. A fishing vessel
c. A vessel towing
d. A vessel motor-sailing

a. Mooring layby for pleasure craft
b. Commercial port ahead
c. Self-propelled ferry
d. Unpowered craft authorised

What does the signal on this vessel mean:

a. Vessel protected against wash, clear channel is shown by a red flag over a white flag
b. Do not pass on either side
c. Pass either side
d. Pilot on board

A vessel showing this signal is:

a. Aground
b. At anchor
c. Carrying dangerous cargo
d. Not under command

Which of the following statements are true:
a. Small Craft are not permitted on Class 1 waterways
b. Small Craft are not permitted on Class 2 waterways
c. Small Craft must always give way to Normal Vessels
d. Small Craft must always carry a pilot

What does this sign mean:

a. No passing or overtaking
b. Two-way traffic
c. Pass port-to-port in this section
d. Do not pass port-to-port in this section

Does this sign on a bridge span mean:

a. Recommended passage two-way traffic
b. Recommended route for Normal Vessels only
c. Recommended route for small vessels only
d. Do not pass under this span

What does this sign mean:

a. Speed limit 12 km/h
b. Speed limit 12 knots
c. Call on VHF channel 12
d. Channel 12m from this sign

On which side should this buoy
be kept when going downstream:

a. To the north
b. To the east
c. To port
d. To starboard

In this situation, involving two Small Craft, which of them should keep clear:

When overtaking in a river, would you pass:

a. After sounding three short blasts
b. On either side of the vessel
c. On the side on which the other vessel is
   displaying a blue board
d. On the side on which you are displaying
   a blue board

A vessel sounding this signal:

a. Is turning to starboard
b. Wishes to overtake to starboard
c. Is indicating that it is unsafe to overtake
d. Is a ferry

Index

Notes

IT'S ALL ABOUT YOU AND THE BOATING YOU DO

RYA MEMBERSHIP APPLICATION

Be part of it

One of boating's biggest attractions is its freedom from rules and regulations. As an RYA member you'll play an active part in keeping it that way, as well as benefiting from free expert advice and information, plus discounts on a wide range of boating products, charts and publications.

To join the RYA, please complete the application form below and send it to The Membership Department, RYA, RYA House, Ensign Way, Hamble, Southampton, Hampshire SO31 4YA. You can also join online at www.rya.org.uk, or by phoning the membership department on +44 (0) 23 8060 4159. Whichever way you choose to apply, you can save money by paying by Direct Debit. A Direct Debit instruction is on the back of this form.

	Title	Forename	Surname	Gender	Date of Birth
Applicant ❶					D D / M M / Y Y Y Y
Applicant ❷					D D / M M / Y Y Y Y
Applicant ❸					D D / M M / Y Y Y Y
Applicant ❹					D D / M M / Y Y Y Y

Address

Post Code

E-mail Applicant ❶	
E-mail Applicant ❷	
E-mail Applicant ❸	
E-mail Applicant ❹	

Home Tel **Day Time Tel** **Mobile Tel**

Type of membership required (Tick Box) – Annual Rate

Junior (0-11)	£5 by direct debit	£5 non direct debit rate
Youth (12-17)	£10 by direct debit	£15 non direct debit rate
Under 25	£20 by direct debit	£25 non direct debit rate
Personal	£40 by direct debit	£45 non direct debit rate
Family*	£60 by direct debit	£65 non direct debit rate

Save money by completing the Direct Debit form overleaf

Please number up to three boating interests in order, with number one being your principal interest

Yacht Racing	Yacht Cruising	Dinghy Racing
Personal Watercraft	Sportboats & RIBs	Windsurfing
Powerboat Racing	Canal Cruising	River Cruising

Dinghy Cruising
Motor Boating

* Family Membership: 2 adults plus any under 18s all living at the same address. Prices valid until 30/9/2013. One discount voucher is accepted for individual memberships, and two discount vouchers are accepted for family membership.

IMPORTANT In order to provide you with membership benefits the details provided by you on this form and in the course of your membership will be maintained on a database. If you do not wish to receive information on member services and benefits please tick here ☐ By applying for membership of the RYA you agree to be bound by the RYA's standard terms and conditions (copies on request or at www.rya.org.uk)

Signature

Date D D / M M / Y Y Y Y

Source Code 0 7 7

Joining Point Code

GET MORE FROM
YOUR
BOATING
SUPPORT THE
RYA

PAY BY DIRECT DEBIT – AND SAVE MONEY

Instructions to your Bank or Building Society to pay by Direct Debit

Please fill in the form and send to:
Membership Department, Royal Yachting Association, RYA House, Ensign Way, Hamble,
Southampton, Hampshire SO31 4YA.

Name and full postal address of your Bank/Building Society

To the Manager _____ Bank/Building Society

Address _____

_____ Postcode _____

Name(s) of Account Holder(s)

_____

Branch Sort Code

| | | — | | | — | | |

Bank/Building Society Account Number

| | | | | | | | |

Originator's Identification Number

| 9 | 5 | 5 | 2 | 1 | 3 |

RYA Membership Number (For office use only)

Instructions to your Bank or Building Society

Please pay Royal Yachting Association Direct Debits from the account detailed in
this instruction subject to the safeguards assured by The Direct Debit Guarantee.
I understand that this instruction may remain with the Royal Yachting Association
and, if so, details will be passed electronically to my Bank/Building Society.

Signature(s)

Date: | D | D | / | M | M | / | Y | Y | Y | Y |

RYA

Be part of it

DIRECT Debit